I0191634

Come close
and
hear me
sing

LizBeth

FLOATING LEAF PRESS

CHARLOTTE, NORTH CAROLINA

Copyright © 2020 by Christa Carter. All rights reserved. With the exception of short quotations for articles and reviews, no part of this publication may be reproduced, transmitted, scanned, distributed, stored in any form or by any means, electronic, mechanical, photocopying, recording, or otherwise, without prior written permission from the author.

My thanks to the editors of Harness Magazine, on whose online website a version of "Yearbook" first appeared.

Published in the United States of America by

FLOATING LEAF PRESS
A division of
WordPlay

Maureen Ryan Griffin
6420 A-1 Rea Road, Suite 218, Charlotte, NC 28277
Phone: 704-494-9961
Email: info@wordplaynow.com
www.wordplaynow.com

1SBN: 978-1-950499-12-0

This book is dedicated
to a life
that brought breath to my soul

Pearl M. Brown

Table of Contents

My silence 7
Naked 8
Have you seen her? 9
Come sit by the stream 10
Familiar 12
At the table 13
Molasses 14
Hot pancakes 15
Is that me or you? 16
Falling 17
Fire 18
Burn 19
Drive 20
Red mud 21
Fluid love 22
Don't leave 23
Pieces of me 24
Yearbook 25
We sit 26
Before 27
Clipboard 28
In a sentimental mood 29
How long does it take to fall out
        of your pattern? 30
Tulips 31
Freedom 32
About the Author 33

My silence

My silence is an invitation to be still. To stay and linger, to remain calm.

My silence is an observance. A chance to see before I act.

My silence is a song. Come close and hear me sing.

Naked

    *I don't undress before you when
I take off my clothes.
    My vulnerability is not my body.
My exposure is not in the words
I speak.
    I am vulnerable and unashamed
in the words I write.*

    *As pen touches paper, I begin to
undress, take off make-up and mask
and I am bare.
    Ink flowing from the pen bleeds
the truth running through my veins.
    No longer hidden but exposed raw.*

*Someone love me, read me,
    naked*

Have you seen her?

I saw her once
by chance

the blued-eyed fox

I've never seen anything like it before
electric red fur
piercing blue eyes
she was wild.

I want to be her

spotted only by a few
who are changed forever when they do

Come sit by the stream

Go to the forest and sit by the stream.

As you come observe your steps
       each one an important reminder
       of the journey.

Take in the sounds as you walk
       A tune full of emotions
         sometimes sad and lonely
       at others
rejoicing with laughter.

As you approach the stream
be still,
catch your breath.
Inhale,
Exhale
Call to mind the journey that brought
you here.

       I'll appear right beside you.

Ready to hear your story;
   how you walked
   through the forest to get to me.

I'll listen
     crying at the parts where it hurt the
most.

I'll offer you this nectar of water
 we'll drink together.

     Sipping, I will sing

This stream of water brings us to life.
We find we are both satisfied,
full from
steadfast love
and faithfulness.

Familiar

I don't know what it is that seems to call forth a familiar; the presence of an old friend

> *Is it my brown skin?*

Is it my curly hair?
> *Is it my big eyes?*

> *Is it the way I talk?*

> *Is it the way I laugh?*

Maybe my smile breaks down barriers we try to erect.

When we met, we were strangers, but by the time we said goodnight,
> *we became familiar*

At the table

Love unfolded at the dinner table
right when the tune of fork and plate
started
you swayed to the movement of wine
in the glass
we were making music long before we
knew the lyrics

Molasses

These words come out slow.
*   Like molasses spilling from the jar.*
I don't know how to make them flow.

Make them taste warm
*   like the first bite of a buttered*
biscuit.
Will they fill you?

Will you go away satisfied?
*   or will you wish you ate the eggs,*
scrambled with cheese?

Hot pancakes

Hot pancakes
Warm two hearts

Teach love is not fluff
With syrup on top

It's "I got the kitchen dirty" batter
Poured with intentionality

A circle flipped to perfection
A covenant

Laid on a plate
Buttered

We eat pancakes for breakfast
Lunch and dinner

Savor each bite like
It is the first

Is that me or you?

Hold up a mirror
Check to see that I still have my eyes
I become like you the closer we get
Taste what you taste
Smell what you smell
Feel what you feel

It scares me
Losing myself to be loved by you

Falling

I can't seem to
catch
the rhythm
 of your
 drum.
I always feel a little
off
beat.
Marching with you,
I seem to
trip over
two
     left
feet.

Fire

Tell me what it's like to be a forest fire
                              wild
              burning

uncontrollable

because I'm a campfire

started for a purpose
              each stick
              laid down
              intentionally

Burn

By morning it's red
It no longer hurts
The scar is forming

I wanted to know you
And Love you too
But I was burning,
Playing with fire

Drive

With a crack in his windshield
He drove me to love

We found God
Traveling on back roads
From death to life

He waved his palm
Across my open wounds
A balm over scars just forming

Red mud

I'm stuck on you
Like red mud on this white truck

We stand out
Call attention to contradiction

I pray you find
These stains look good on you

Fluid love

You can cry in my lap

You can spit in my face

You can give me a sweaty embrace

For I will collect it all
to feel baptized in love

Don't leave

I see it starting to leave you.
You can't even walk straight.
The high from last night is
no longer holding you up.

Aimlessly you roam the block
looking for something
anything
That will hold you up again;
something
that won't leave you

Alone

Pieces of me

*I'm desperate to find the pieces I hid
from you
I knew one day I would need payment
for all the things I said
        Promises I couldn't keep
        Attention I didn't give
Forgive me for the times I was devoted
to myself more than you
        I devoured your love*

*Sated,
And now all I have
        are the pieces of me*

Yearbook

Sign your yearbook
to remind you of how we loved

how we journeyed through the slow
unassuming change of seasons

in December I came to rest
my head on your pillow

used your body to keep me warm
winter was too cold

we laid down soil
for flowers to bloom in spring

our garden grew out of love
and in the summer, we laughed

as the leaves changed
and the air cleared

we knew what it meant
to be loved

We sit

We sit
cuddled between

      a Past less than Perfect
  and
      a Progressive Present

knowing the Future
holds only

    memories

Before

I want things to go back to how they were before.
            We both do.
But we remind each other of just how fragile we are, how brokenness really works and some pieces never seem to connect   again.

Clipboard

*That morning I walked in
the room was a mess
she was gone*

*She knew it was coming
heard the glass break before
I could try
to put us back together*

*Clean up the chaos
left in her absence
wipe the table with tears*

*I want her back
long enough to reclaim the secrets she
kept*

In a sentimental mood**

The radio plays In a sentimental mood
          She listens

*On her plate, she separates the broccoli
and corn*
          She looks

Can two unlikely things fall in love?
          She thinks

Alone at a table for two
          She is silent

If I had one more chance
          I would say

"I loved you on purpose"

**"In a Sentimental Mood" song title by
Duke Ellington

How long does it take to fall out of your pattern?

I keep tracing my hand on your print
like I don't know what's coming next
like I don't know that around the
corner is
          a ghost
a resurrection
          a pattern I still find beautiful

Tulips

Draw tulips to house this memory

A single sunflower that smiles

Rose petals envelop
the way you laugh at my jokes

Take a sip of water to catch your breath

I could fill a garden with moments like
these.

Freedom

This is the way to freedom
honeyed
messy
sweet

You won't find it across continents
or in the zeal of a sword

It's a parable
like in the beginning God created
your palpitating heart
it swoons to the tune
of his handcrafted music box

But when the metronome stops
it's hard to find the beat
You feel lost as if
someone stole the music sheet

The chords changed
instead you learned a new song

About the Author

All LizBeth poetry is written by Christa Elizabeth Carter. As a poet, Christa strives to express the poetry of life observed—how we live and love, how we thrive and survive. If only for two lines, may a reader feel a shared connection. She resides in Durham, NC, and enjoys quality time with friends.

*** special thanks to family and friends who have encouraged me to keep writing, encouraged me to keep living. ***

www.ingramcontent.com/pod-product-compliance
Lightning Source LLC
Chambersburg PA
CBHW020037040426
42331CB00031B/974